A big hit

Nat gets a bat.

Up, up, up.

It is a big hit.

Dan runs to get it.

Dan hits his leg on the log.

10

Sam runs to get it.

Sam runs into the bin.

Pam gets it.

Before reading

Say the sounds: g o b h e r f u l

Practise blending the sounds: hit bat runs leg log bin Nat Sam Pam Dan gets hits

High-frequency words: big up it on am get

Tricky words: to the I is his into

Vocabulary check: bin – This is something you put your rubbish in.

Story discussion: Look at the cover. What game do you think the children are playing? What equipment do you need? What do you do in this game?

Teaching points: Introduce the new tricky word "into". Ask children if they can say "to" without sounding it out. Remind them that the tricky part is the "o". It doesn't correspond with the sound /o/ as in "dog". Bring "in" and "to" together for children to say. Explain that "into" is a compound word made from two smaller words. It is also a two-syllable word.

After reading

Comprehension:
- Who was batting in the game and who was bowling?
- What happened to Dan when he ran for the ball?
- What happened to Sam when he tried to get the ball?
- What did Pam do?

Fluency: Speed read the words again from the inside front cover.